TREASURY OF LITERATURE

JUMP RIGHT IN

SENIOR AUTHORS
ROGER C. FARR
DOROTHY S. STRICKLAND

AUTHORS
RICHARD F. ABRAHAMSON
ELLEN BOOTH CHURCH
BARBARA BOWEN COULTER
BERNICE E. CULLINAN
MARGARET A. GALLEGO
W. DORSEY HAMMOND
JUDITH L. IRVIN
KAREN KUTIPER
DONNA M. OGLE
TIMOTHY SHANAHAN
PATRICIA SMITH
JUNKO YOKOTA
HALLIE KAY YOPP

SENIOR CONSULTANTS
ASA G. HILLIARD III
JUDY M. WALLIS

CONSULTANTS
ALONZO A. CRIM
ROLANDO R. HINOJOSA-SMITH
LEE BENNETT HOPKINS
ROBERT J. STERNBERG

HARCOURT BRACE & COMPANY
Orlando Atlanta Austin Boston San Francisco Chicago Dallas New York
Toronto London

ISBN 0-15-301248-X

6 7 8 9 10   032 97 96 95

Acknowledgments

For permission to reprint copyrighted material, grateful acknowledgment is made to the following sources:

Childrens Press, Inc.: Cover illustration by Anne Sikorski from *City Mouse and Country Mouse* by Patricia and Fredrick McKissack. Copyright © 1985 by Regensteiner Publishing Enterprises, Inc.

Aileen Fisher: "All That Sky" from *Out in the Dark and Daylight* by Aileen Fisher. Text copyright © 1980 by Aileen Fisher. "Baby Chick" from *Runny Days, Sunny Days* by Aileen Fisher. Text copyright © 1958 by Aileen Fisher; text copyright renewed © 1986 by Aileen Fisher.

Greenwillow Books, a division of William Morrow & Company, Inc.: *What Game Shall We Play?* by Pat Hutchins. Copyright © 1990 by Pat Hutchins. *I Wish I Could Fly* by Ron Maris. Copyright © 1986 by Ron Maris. Cover illustration by Jose Aruego and Ariane Dewey from *One Duck, Another Duck* by Charlotte Pomerantz. Illustration copyright © 1984 by Jose Aruego and Ariane Dewey. *Flap Your Wings and Try* by Charlotte Pomerantz, illustrated by Nancy Tafuri. Text copyright © 1989 by Charlotte Pomerantz; illustrations copyright © 1989 by Nancy Tafuri.

Harcourt Brace & Company: Cover illustration from *Feathers for Lunch* by Lois Ehlert. Copyright © 1990 by Lois Ehlert.

HarperCollins Publishers: "Wouldn't You?" from *You Read to Me, I'll Read to You* by John Ciardi. Text copyright © 1962 by John Ciardi. *Bet You Can't* by Penny Dale. Copyright © 1987 by Penny Dale. Cover illustration by Crockett Johnson from *The Carrot Seed* by Ruth Krauss. Illustration copyright 1945 by Crockett Johnson.

Robert B. Luce, Inc.: "Point to the Right" from *Let's Do Fingerplays!* (Retitled: "Where To Look") by Marion F. Grayson. Text copyright © 1962 by Marion F. Grayson.

Macmillan Publishing Company, a Division of Macmillan, Inc.: *The Chick and the Duckling* by Mirra Ginsburg, illustrated by Jose Aruego and Ariane Dewey. Text copyright © 1972 by Mirra Ginsburg; illustrations copyright © 1972 by Jose Aruego and Ariane Dewey.

G. P. Putnam's Sons, a division of The Putnam & Grosset Group: Cover illustration from *Jen the Hen* by Colin and Jacqui Hawkins. Copyright © 1985 by Colin and Jacqui Hawkins.

Illustration Credits

Key: (t) top, (b) bottom, (c) center.

Table of Contents Art
Thomas Vroman Associates, Inc., 4, 5

Bookshelf Art
Thomas Vroman Associates, Inc., 6, 7

Theme Opening Art
Diane Patterson 8, 9; Sue Parnell, 64, 65

Selection Art
Pat Hutchins, 10–32; Loretta Krupinski, 34–39; Ron Maris, 40–62; Nancy Tafuri, 66–88; Sylvie Daigneault, 90–101; Jose Aruego and Ariane Dewey, 102–119

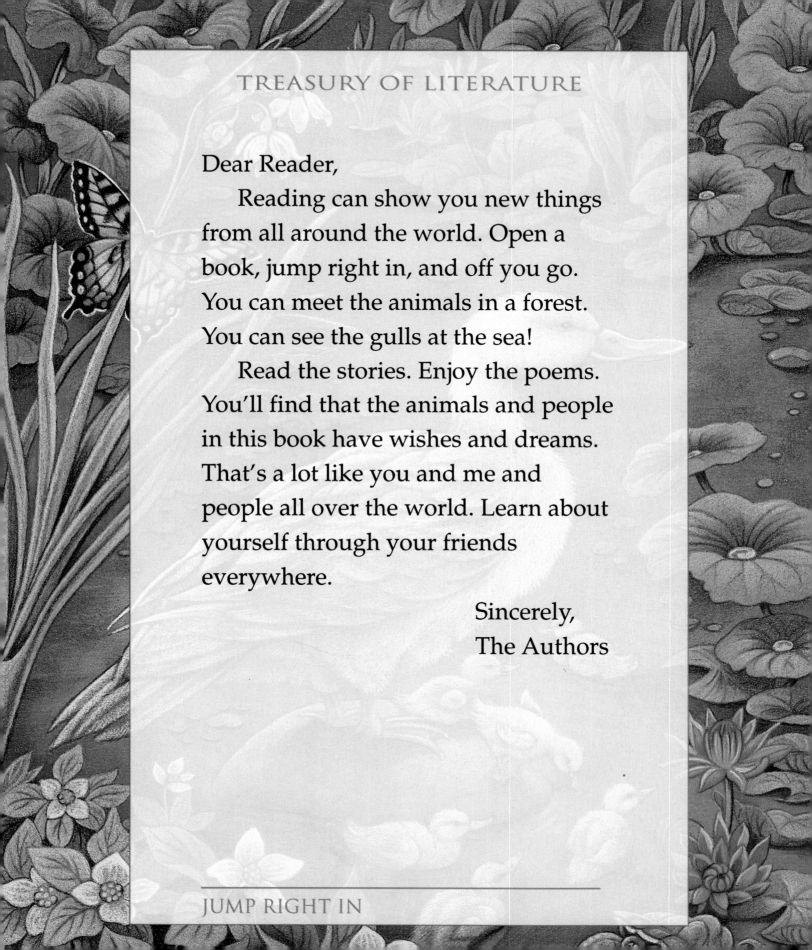

Dear Reader,

Reading can show you new things from all around the world. Open a book, jump right in, and off you go. You can meet the animals in a forest. You can see the gulls at the sea!

Read the stories. Enjoy the poems. You'll find that the animals and people in this book have wishes and dreams. That's a lot like you and me and people all over the world. Learn about yourself through your friends everywhere.

Sincerely,
The Authors

CONTENTS

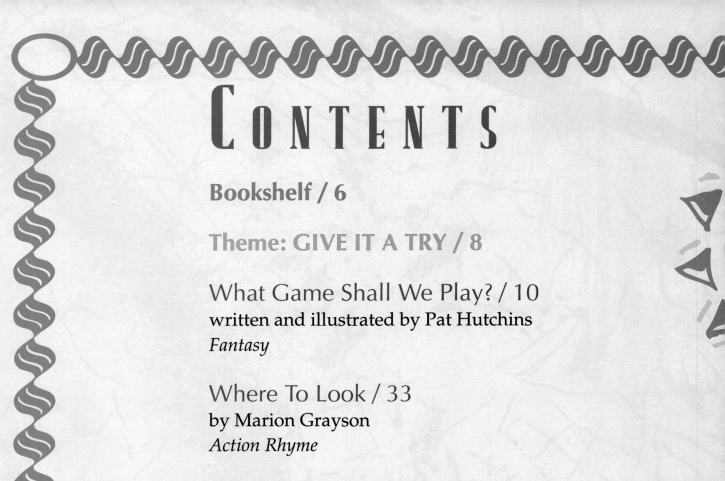

BOOKSHELF

ONE DUCK, ANOTHER DUCK

by Charlotte Pomerantz

An owl named Danny goes to the pond with his grandmother. Danny tries to count the ducks. "One duck, another duck," he says. Count the ducks with Danny.

Award-Winning Author

Harcourt Brace Library Book

JEN THE HEN

by Colin and Jacqui Hawkins

Jen the hen is very clever. She writes a letter for Ken and Ben and gives it to Wren. Will Wren be able to find Ken and Ben?

Award-Winning Authors

Harcourt Brace Library Book

6

COUNTRY MOUSE AND CITY MOUSE

by Patricia and Fredrick McKissack

Would you rather have an old, small house or a big, new house? Visit both kinds with Country Mouse and City Mouse so you can choose.

THE CARROT SEED

by Ruth Krauss

A boy plants a carrot seed. He is sure it will grow. His family tells him, "It won't come up." What do you think will happen?

Award-Winning Author

FEATHERS FOR LUNCH

by Lois Ehlert

What do you think a cat should eat? Find out if the hungry cat in this book will be happy with feathers for lunch.

Caldecott Honor Book,

Outstanding Science Trade Book,

Teachers' Choice

8

THEME

Give It a Try

What do you wish you could do?
Is there anything new you'd like to try?
See if these stories give you some ideas.

CONTENTS

9

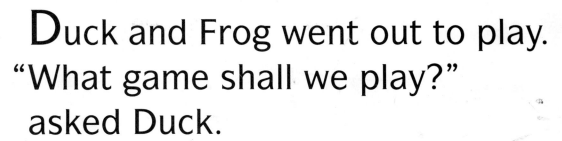

Duck and Frog went out to play.
"What game shall we play?"
asked Duck.
"I don't know," said Frog.
"Let's go and ask Fox."

11

So off they went to look for Fox.
Duck looked across the fields,
but he wasn't there.

Frog looked among the tall grass,

13

and there he was.

"What game shall we play, Fox?"
they asked.
"I don't know," said Fox.
"Let's go and ask Mouse."

So off they went to look for Mouse.
Duck looked over the wall,
but Mouse wasn't there.
Frog looked under the wall,
but she wasn't there, either.

So Fox looked in the wall,

and there she was.

"What game shall we play, Mouse?"
they asked.
"I don't know," said Mouse.
"Let's go and ask Rabbit."

So off they went to look for Rabbit.
Duck looked near his hole,
Frog looked on top of the hole,
Fox looked around the hole,

and Mouse looked in the hole,

and there he was.

"What game shall we play,
Rabbit?" they asked.
"I don't know," said Rabbit.
"Let's go and ask Squirrel."

So off they went to look for Squirrel.
Duck looked behind the tree,
Frog looked in front of the tree,
Fox looked up to the top of the tree,
Mouse looked under the tree,

and Rabbit looked
through the leaves
of the tree,

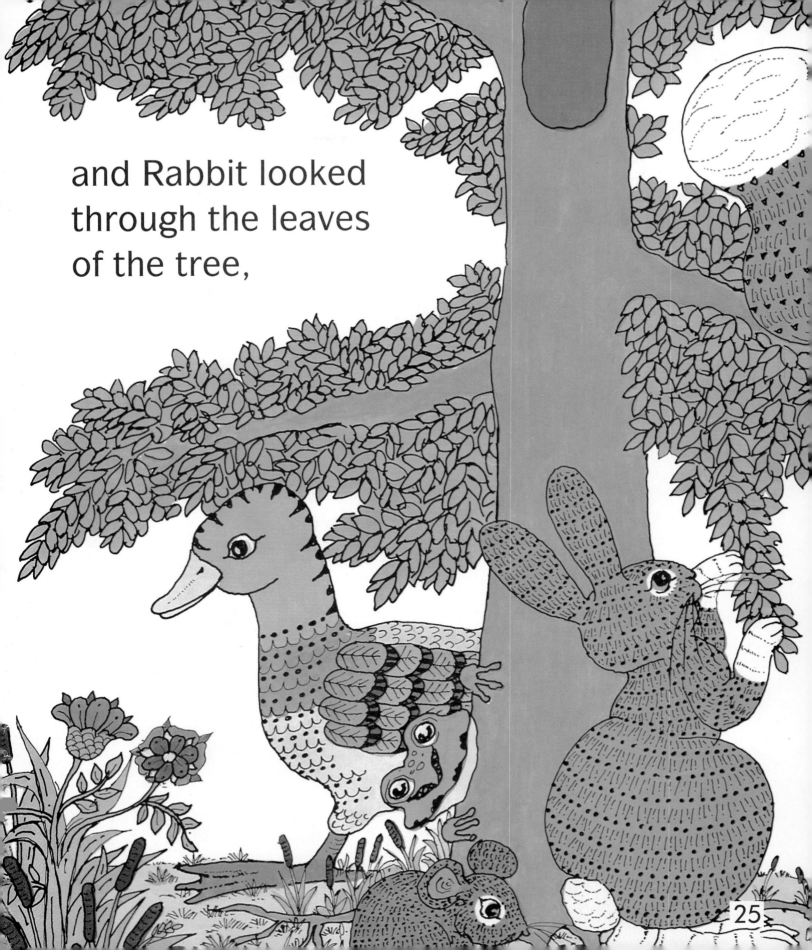

and there she was.

"What game shall we play, Squirrel?"
they asked.
"I don't know," said Squirrel.
"Let's find Owl and ask him."

But Owl found them first.
"What game shall we play, Owl?"
they asked.
"Hide and seek," said Owl.

And while Owl closed his eyes,
Duck and Frog hid in the pond,
Fox hid in the long grass,
Mouse hid in the wall,
Rabbit hid in the hole,
and Squirrel hid in the leaves
in the tree.

Then Owl went to look for them.

Where To Look

An action rhyme
by Marion Grayson

Look to the right of me,
Look to the left of me,
Look up above me,
Look down below.
Right, left, up,
And down so slow.

33

Where Is Thumbkin?

A traditional song

Where is Thumbkin?

Where is Thumbkin?

Here I am.

Here I am.

How are you this morning?

I am fine, thank you.

Walk away.

Walk away.

illustrated by Loretta Krupinski

34

Where is Pointer?

Where is Pointer?

Here I am.

Here I am.

How are you this morning?

I am fine, thank you.

Hop away.

Hop away.

Where is tall man?
Where is tall man?
Here I am.
Here I am.
How are you this morning?
I am fine, thank you.
Jump away.
Jump away.

Where is ring man?
Where is ring man?
Here I am.
Here I am.
How are you this morning?
I am fine, thank you.
Run away.
Run away.

Where is small man?
Where is small man?
Here I am.
Here I am.
How are you this morning?
I am fine, thank you.
Run away.
Run away.

Where are all the men?
Where are all the men?
Here we are.
Here we are.
How are you this morning?
We are fine, thank you.
Run away.
Run away.

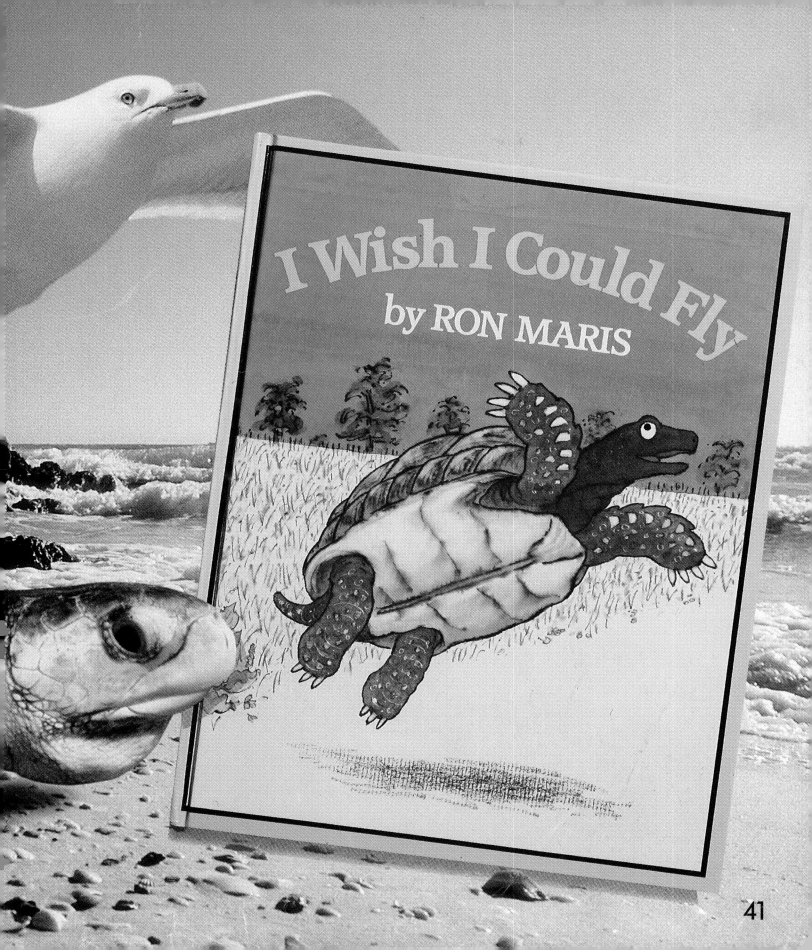

I Wish I Could Fly

by RON MARIS

"Good morning, Bird.

I wish I could fly like you."

CRASH! BANG!
WALLOP! CRUNCH!

47

"Hello, Frog.
I wish I could dive
like you."

FLOP! PLOP!
SPLUTTER! SPLASH!

"How are you, Squirrel?
I wish I could climb
like you."

WIBBLE! WOBBLE!
WRIGGLE! ROCK!

"Good day, Rabbit.
I wish I could run like you."

**PUFF! PANT!
STAGGER! GASP!**

"I can't fly like Bird,
I can't dive like Frog,
I can't climb like Squirrel,
I can't run like Rabbit,
but...

"When it rains,
I don't get wet.
I'm **SNUG**, **WARM**,
COZY, and **DRY!**"

Wouldn't You?

If I

Could go

As high

And low

As the wind

As the wind

As the wind

Can blow—

I'd go!

John Ciardi

WHEATFIELD WITH A LARK (1887)
Vincent van Gogh (1853–1890), Dutch
Rijksmuseum, Amsterdam

T H E M E

On Our Own

How many things can you do on your own? Do you think it's fun to learn new things? Read about animals and people who do things on their own.

C O N T E N T S

65

FLAP YOUR WINGS AND TRY

BY CHARLOTTE POMERANTZ
ILLUSTRATED BY NANCY TAFURI

I'm a little baby bird
Wondering how to fly.
See my Grandma in the sky,
Why can't I, can't I?

See my Grandpa in the sky,
Why can't I, can't I?
Mommy whispers, Hushaby,
By and by you'll fly.

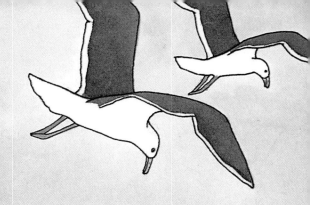

Daddy sings a lullaby,
By and by and by.

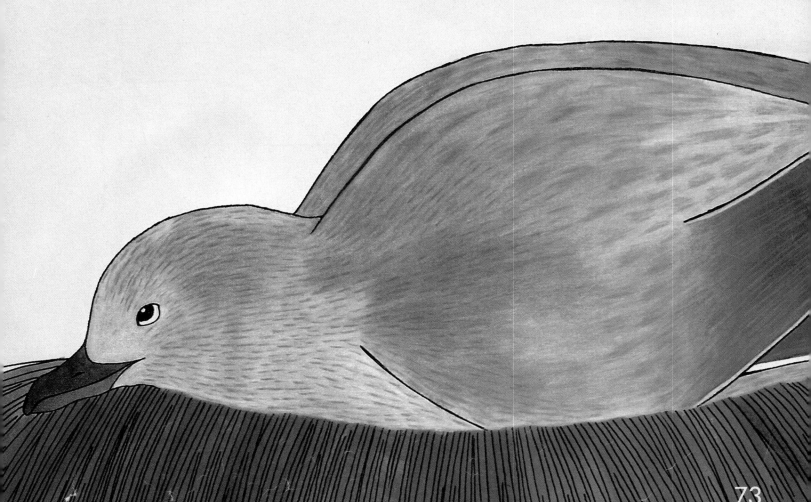

Sister says, Why don't you try?
Flap your wings and try.
So I flap my wings
and try,

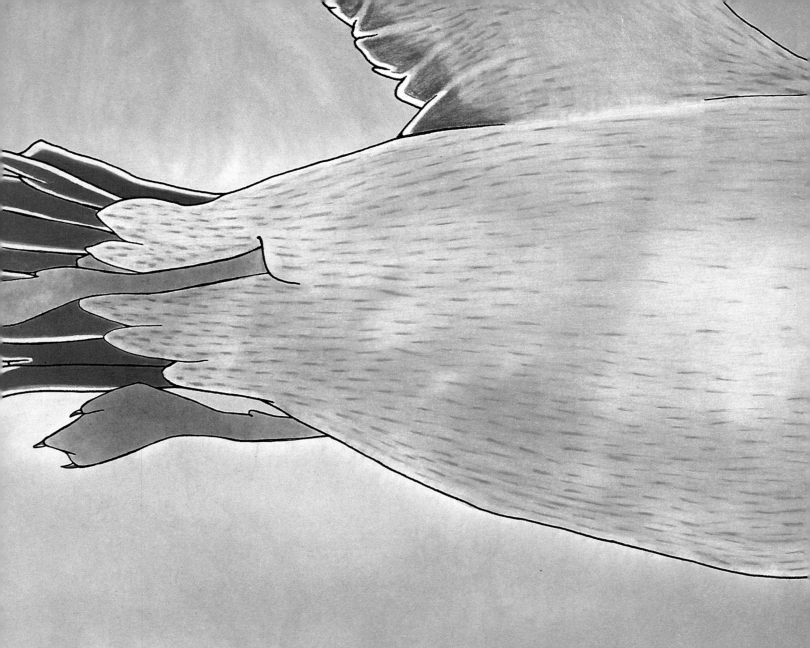

And soon I'm in the sky!
Look at me, way up high,
I can fly, can fly!

Below me is a baby bird.
She sees me in the sky.
I can almost hear her sigh,
Why can't I, can't I?

Down,
     down,
          down, way down I fly
And say, Why don't you try?

I watch her flap her wings
and try,

And soon she's in the sky!
Look at us, way up high,
We can fly, can fly!

Below us baby birds call, Why,
Why can't I, can't I?
Hush, we tell them, Hushaby,
You will fly, will fly.

You will fly,
by and by,
by and by and by.

All That Sky

by Aileen Fisher

Wouldn't you think
the birds that fly
would lose their way
in *all that sky?*

Six Little Ducks

A traditional song

Illustrated by

Sylvie Daigneault

Six little ducks
went swimming one day,
Over the pond and far away.

Mother duck said,
"Quack, quack, quack."
And five little ducks
came swimming right back.

Five little ducks
went swimming one day,
Over the pond and far away.

Mother duck said,
"Quack, quack, quack."
And four little ducks
came swimming right back.

Four little ducks
went swimming one day,
Over the pond and far away.

Mother duck said,
"Quack, quack, quack."
And three little ducks
came swimming right back.

Three little ducks
went swimming one day,
Over the pond and far away.

Mother duck said,
"Quack, quack, quack."
And two little ducks
came swimming right back.

Two little ducks
went swimming one day,
Over the pond and far away.

Mother duck said,
"**Quack, quack, quack.**"
And one little duck
came swimming right back.

One little duck
went swimming one day,
Over the pond and far away.

Mother duck said,
"Quack, quack, quack."
And no little ducks
came swimming right back.

The Chick
and the Duckling

Translated from the Russian of V. Suteyev.

by Mirra Ginsburg
Pictures by Jose Aruego & Ariane Dewey

Aladdin Books

102

A Duckling came out
of the shell.
"I am out!" he said.

"Me too," said the Chick.

"I am taking a walk,"
said the Duckling.

"Me too," said the Chick.

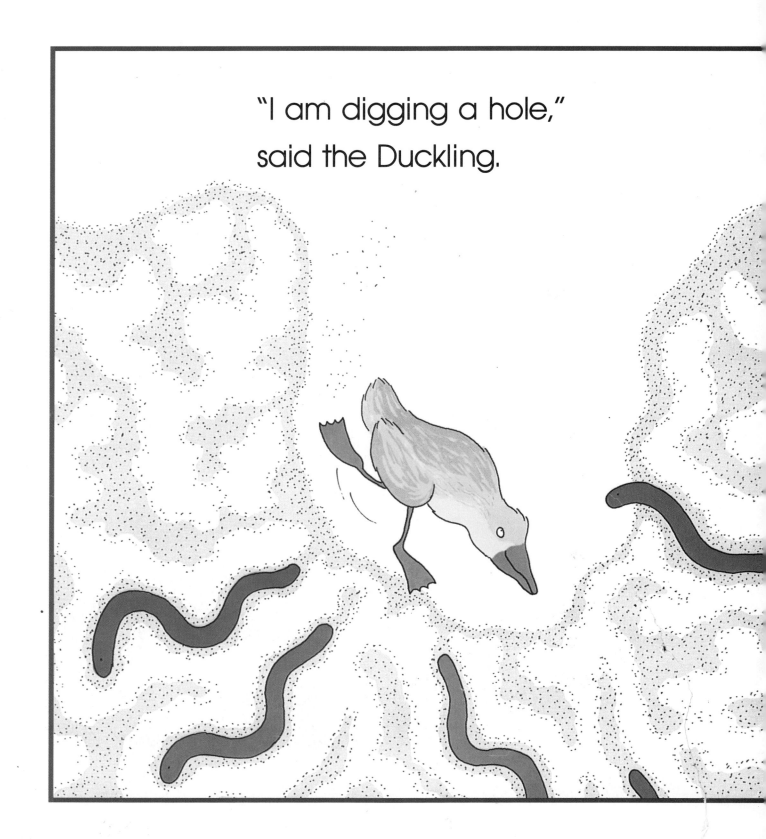

"I am digging a hole,"
said the Duckling.

"Me too,"
said the Chick.

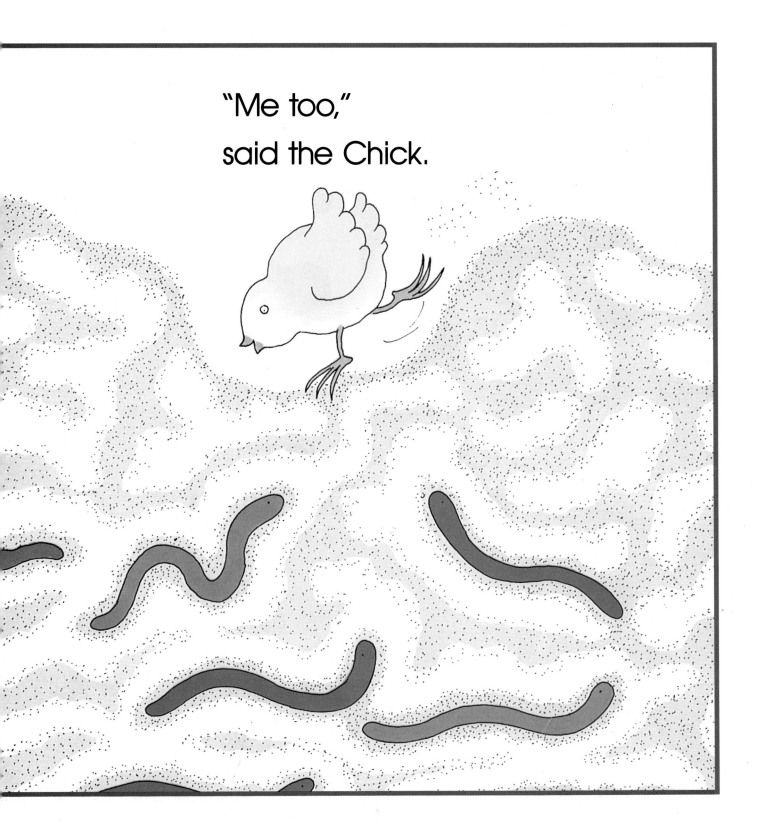

"I found a worm,"
said the Duckling.

"Me too,"
said the Chick.

"I caught
a butterfly,"
said the
Duckling.

"Me too,"
said the Chick.

"I am going for a swim,"
said the Duckling.

"Me too,"
said the Chick.

"I am swimming,"
said the Duckling.

"Me too!"
cried the Chick.

The Duckling pulled
the Chick out.

"I'm going for
another swim,"
said the Duckling.

"Not me,"
said the Chick.

Baby

by Aileen Fisher

Peck
    peck
    peck
on the warm brown egg.
OUT comes a neck.
OUT comes a leg.

Chick

How
   does
     a chick
who's not been about,
discover the trick
of how to get out?

BET YOU CAN'T

Penny Dale

131

135